QUEEN

THE FULL PICTURE

B L O O M S B U R Y

QUEEN

THE FULL PICTURE

**BY THEIR OFFICIAL TOUR
PHOTOGRAPHER DENIS O'REGAN**

A percentage of the royalty earnings
from this book will be donated to the
Rainbow Trust, a charity for family-
centred care for children with life-
threatening or terminal illness.

First published in Great Britain 1995
Bloomsbury Publishing Plc, 2 Soho
Square, London W1V 6HB

Additional photography by Richard
Young and Brian Rasic

ISBN 0 7475 2475 0

10 9 8 7 6 5 4 3 2 1

Designed by Bradbury and Williams
Printed by Butler and Tanner Limited,
Frome and London

INTRODUCTION

I first saw Queen in 1973, supporting Mott the Hoople at the Hammersmith Odeon in London, and I marvelled at the pretentiousness and confidence of their lead singer. I would soon learn to arrive at concerts late enough to bypass support acts – but in doing so I may have deprived myself of other opportunities to witness history being made, as I had surely done with Queen.

I was not yet a professional photographer, but I had borrowed my uncle's camera earlier that year to photograph David Bowie as Aladdin Sane, also at the Odeon. In those days, security was non-existent – all I had to do was buy a ticket, rush down to the front with the rest of the audience, and jump into the orchestra pit. This pit has long since become part of the stage.

Following the success of 'Killer Queen', and having watched Queen's frontman develop into a star performer, I felt the urge to photograph such a visually stunning band, and again borrowed the trusty Halina. I trekked back to the Hammersmith Odeon for the 1975 Christmas show.

A few days later I took my photographs to Queen's management in South Audley Street, and, after blundering into the wrong office, I asked a young man

for directions, knowing full well that I was talking to Elton John. I kept my cool and followed his directions down to the correct department. There I was referred to *Jackie* magazine, who bought a picture for £12 – my first ever sale.

The punk explosion followed soon afterwards, with its new icons attacking groups like Queen for the extravagance of their music and presentation. The band countered this by undertaking a tour that brought them back from the overwhelming scale of their 1976 free concert in front of 150,000 in Hyde Park to the relative intimacy of the Lyceum Ballroom in London, where they performed with a reduced lighting rig and stage.

I was as yet unable to gain official access to bands such as Queen, and punk gave me the opportunity to serve my photographic apprenticeship in venues such as the Marquee and the Rock Garden, taking pictures of nascent stars like the young punks Adam Ant and Billy Idol, as well as the Police and Dire Straits. At the end of it all, Queen emerged from the seventies unscathed and bigger than ever, and I had built up a reputation which would in the future allow me to photograph bands of greater stature than before.

Queen's appeal seemed all-encompassing. On record their music was diverse, ranging from delicate ballads through pastiche to heavy rock. The band's expertise as songwriters and musicians was without question, and this was more than apparent in their live performances. The albums were well produced, but the live concerts were absolutely spectacular, and took Queen beyond the bands of their era in terms of both the entire show and Freddie's performance.

Freddie would strut across the stage, whipping and stabbing with his unique sawn-off microphone stand, giving the songs everything he had, yet exciting and manipulating the audience at the same time. At the end of a song he would often stand motionless and simply stare at them, wringing from them every last drop of applause. At some point in the show he would cement his hold over them by first chatting cheekily, then indulging in a communal sound check, dragging the audience through the vocal scales until they could go no further. At this point they were his, and the band would launch into the next song. Very few singers could gain such control over a crowd; it was a joy to watch.

I followed Queen in an unofficial capacity for a number of years,

photographing them on almost every tour, and watching them develop into what was for me the greatest rock band ever, who finally proved it to the world at Wembley Stadium during Live Aid in 1985. They were invigorated by that experience, and seemed also to have proved something to themselves – that they were powerful, talented and professional performers, who could take on any audience in any venue.

In the early eighties I toured the world as official photographer with David Bowie, the Rolling Stones and Duran Duran, among others, and in 1986 Queen took me on their last tour around Europe, which set a German attendance record of over 80,000 at Mannheim, and a record 80,000 at Budapest's Nepstadion. They unbelievably followed up two Wembley Stadium shows with the record-breaking last ever Queen show in front of a crowd of 150,000 at Knebworth – the largest paying audience ever in Britain. They had taken rock music to Hungary, performing the first open-air concert behind the Iron Curtain, at a time when no one knew that the curtain was about to fall – both on Communism and, sadly, on Queen in concert.

DENIS O'REGAN, August 1995

THE
E
Y

ARLY
EARS

IN 1973 I
BORROWED MY
UNCLE'S CAMERA,
TOOK A BUS TO
THE HAMMERSMITH
ODEON, AND RAN
DOWN TO THE
FRONT OF THE
THEATRE TO TAKE
THESE, THE FIRST
PICTURES I EVER
SOLD. AT THIS
POINT, SUCH AN
ELABORATE LIGHT
SHOW HAD NEVER
BEEN SEEN, AND AS
FOR FREDDIE...

The SHOW WAS
BROADCAST ON
TELEVISION ON
CHRISTMAS EVE.

QUEEN
12

BACKSTAGE AT A
KANSAS AFTER-
SHOW PARTY IN
LONDON. KANSAS
HAD REPLACED
QUEEN ON A
1974 AMERICAN
MOTT THE HOOPLE
TOUR AFTER BRIAN
HAD FALLEN ILL,
CAUSING THEM TO
PULL OUT.

IN THE EARLY
YEARS, FREDDIE'S
STAGE OUTFITS
WEREN'T
CONSIDERED TO
BE EXCESSIVELY
OUTRAGEOUS,
SINCE QUEEN
EMERGED IN THE
GLAM ROCK ERA
OF THE SEVENTIES
ALONGSIDE THE
LIKES OF DAVID
BOWIE, GARY
GLITTER AND
SLADE.

EVEN IN THE LATE
SEVENTIES, AS
PUNK TOOK A
GRIP OF CLUBS
ALL OVER THE UK,
FREDDIE IGNORED
THE VAGARIES OF
THE LATEST
FASHIONS AND
HIS DRESS
BECAME, IF
ANYTHING, EVEN
MORE
FLAMBOYANT.

ROGER TAYLOR ON DRUMS: THE ROCK STAR OF THE BAND OFF STAGE, AND A POWERFUL PERFORMER ON STAGE, HE WROTE THE MASSIVE EIGHTIES HITS 'A KIND OF MAGIC' AND 'RADIO GAGA'.

BRIAN'S UNIQUE
SOUND MAY IN
PART BE ATTRIBUTED
TO HIS PLECTRUM –
A PRE-DECIMAL
CURRENCY
SIXPENNY PIECE!
HIS FIRST GUITAR
WAS MADE BY HIS
FATHER FROM AN
OLD FIREPLACE.

AT THE HYDE
PARK CONCERT IN
1976, I WAS STILL
A FAN TAKING
ADVANTAGE OF
LAX SECURITY,
AND WAS
ACTUALLY
STANDING NEXT
TO FREDDIE AS HE
CLIMBED INTO THE
LIFT THAT WOULD
CARRY HIM UP TO
THE STAGE IN A
CLOUD OF SMOKE,
TO SING 'NOW
I'M HERE' IN
FRONT OF THE
ESTIMATED
CROWD OF
150,000.

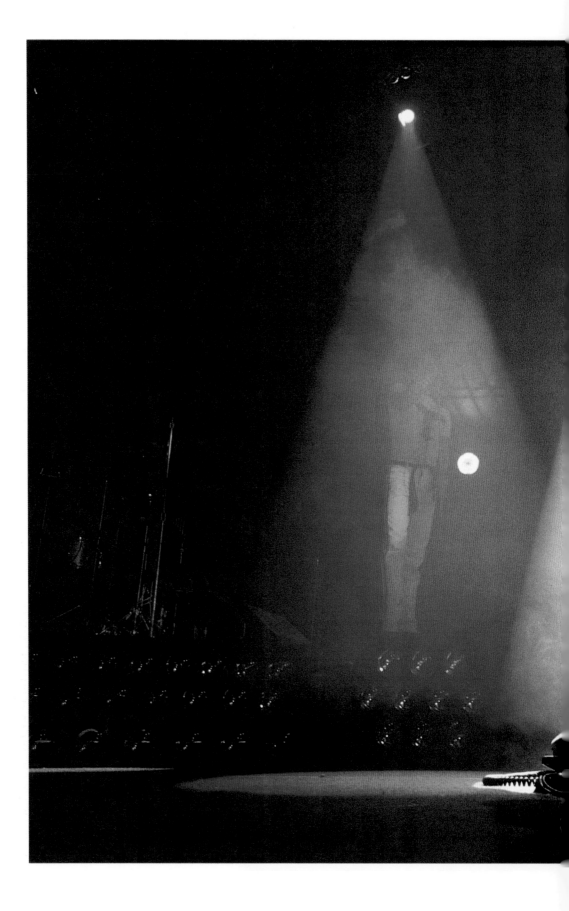

BRIAN WOULD
TAKE GUITAR
VIRTUOSITY TO
NEW HEIGHTS WITH
HIS SOLO DURING
'BRIGHTON ROCK',
SENDING THE
SOUND SWEEPING
BACKWARDS AND
FORWARDS ACROSS
THE STAGE.

PART OF THE 1979 RETURN TO THE SMALLER VENUES, WHERE FREDDIE RENEWED CONTACT WITH THE AUDIENCE. AT THE LYCEUM BALLROOM IN LONDON, THE LIGHTING RIG WAS REDUCED TO FIT IN THE THEATRE AND THE SHOW OPENED WITH A FRENETIC 'WE WILL ROCK YOU'.

'TIE YOUR
MOTHER DOWN',
ONE OF QUEEN'S
EARLY ROCKERS,
WAS OFTEN THE
FIRST SONG IN
THE SET TO
TRANSFORM THE
AUDIENCE INTO A
SWAYING MASS.

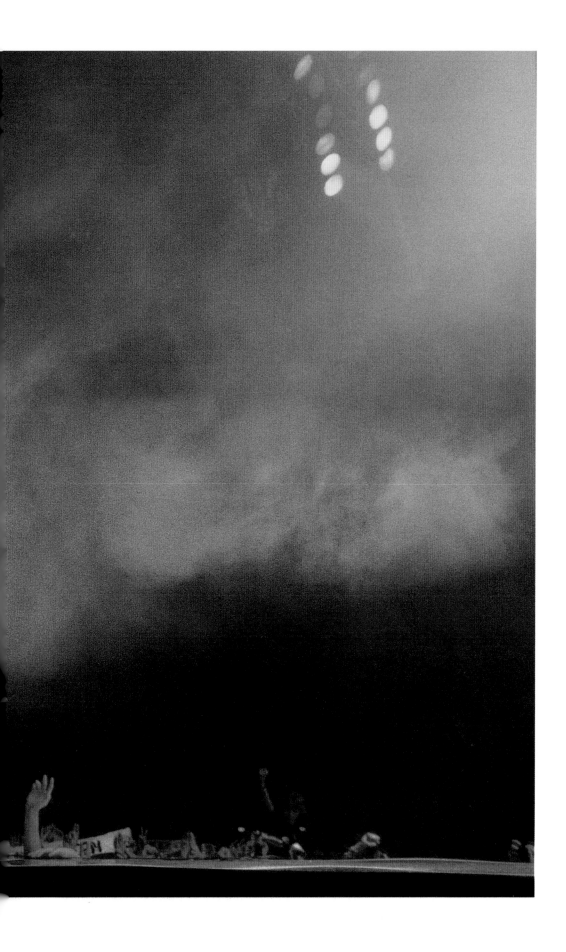

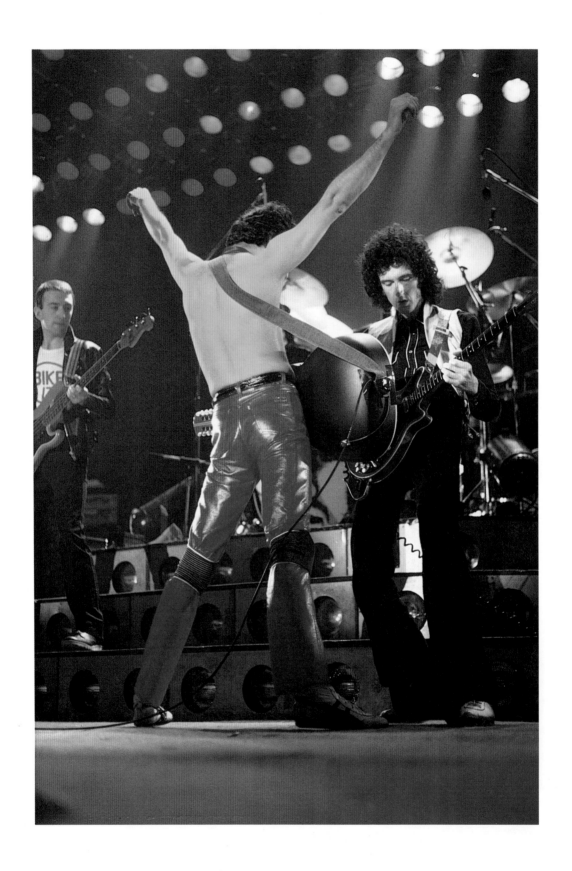

QUEEN PLAY THE MANCHESTER APOLLO.

I ENCOUNTERED
THIS SUPERMAN
AGAIN TEN YEARS
LATER ON
ANOTHER TOUR,
WHERE HE TURNED
UP AS DURAN
DURAN'S SECURITY
– MINUS THE
TIGHTS AND
UNDERPANTS!

AS THE BAND LEFT
THE STAGE, THE
LIGHTING RIG
MOVED UPWARDS
AND TURNED TO
FACE THE AUDIENCE,
ACCOMPANIED BY
QUEEN'S RENDITION
OF 'GOD SAVE THE
QUEEN'.

AS BRIAN TOOK
HIS ACOUSTIC
GUITAR TO THE
STOOL AT THE
FRONT OF THE
STAGE, THE
CROWD KNEW IT
MEANT 'LOVE OF
MY LIFE'.

THE

SE

DEC

COND

ADE

FREDDIE COULD RELAX AS THE AUDIENCE, NO MATTER WHAT THEIR NATIVE TONGUE, TOOK OVER THE SINGING OF 'LOVE OF MY LIFE'. FOR MANY FANS, QUEEN'S LYRICS WERE THE QUICKEST ROUTE TO LEARNING TO SPEAK ENGLISH.

BRIAN MAY AS A
CHARACTER IS
RESERVED, BUT HE
HAD A HEAVY
ROCK INFLUENCE
ON QUEEN'S
MUSIC, WITH
SONGS SUCH AS
'WE WILL ROCK
YOU', 'NOW I'M
HERE', 'HAMMER
TO FALL' AND THE
THEME FOR THE
FILM *FLASH
GORDON*.

IN 1982 QUEEN
BEGAN THEIR
JOURNEY INTO
OUTDOOR
STADIUMS IN
EUROPE BY
PLAYING BRITISH
FOOTBALL
GROUNDS AND
THE MILTON
KEYNES BOWL.

'GET DOWN MAKE LOVE' INTRODUCED MORE SUBTLE LIGHTING INTO A SHOW AS THE SPOTLIGHTS SWOOPED AROUND THE STAGE ACCOMPANYING BAYING GUITARS AND SOUND EFFECTS.

**FREDDIE'S
MOVEMENTS ON
STAGE WERE
OFTEN BALLETIC,
ADAPTED FOR A
ROCK AUDIENCE.**

QUEEN HAD FIRST COME TO PROMINENCE IN THE EARLY SEVENTIES, AS SUPPORT ACT TO MOTT THE HOOPLE. YEARS LATER, THE HOOPLE'S KEYBOARD PLAYER MORGAN FISHER BRIEFLY JOINED QUEEN'S LINE-UP, BUT IT WASN'T TO LAST.

AS FREDDIE
MATURED, HE
ADAPTED HIS
ONSTAGE
PERSONA,
INCORPORATING
THE 'CLONE' LOOK
INTO HIS
WARDOBE AND
ABANDONING THE
EARLIER
OSTENTATIOUS
COSTUMES IN
FAVOUR OF
SIMPLER JEANS
AND T-SHIRTS.

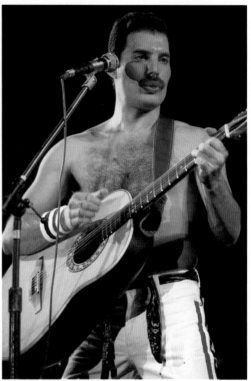

FREDDIE WOULD
TAKE THE
ACOUSTIC GUITAR
SPOT FOR 'CRAZY
LITTLE THING
CALLED LOVE'
AND AWAIT THE
AUDIENCE'S ROAR
OF 'READY
FREDDIE' DURING
THE CHORUS.

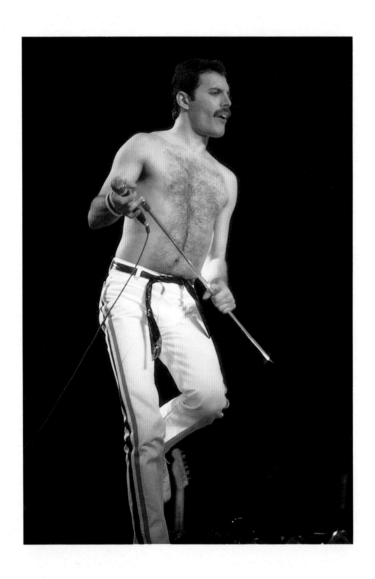

**BECAUSE FREDDIE
RARELY STOOD
STILL ON STAGE, HE
DIDN'T NEED A
CONVENTIONAL
MICROPHONE
STAND. INSTEAD
HIS UBIQUITOUS
PROP WAS A MORE
MANŒUVRABLE
'SAWN-OFF'
MODEL, UNIQUE TO
HIS PERFORMING
STYLE, WHICH HE
USED CONSTANTLY,
ALMOST LIKE A
CHEERLEADER'S
BATON – OR
SOMETIMES A
SURROGATE
GUITAR.**

LIKE THE REST OF
THE BAND, FREDDIE
TOOK HIS
INSPIRATION FROM
THE AUDIENCE,
CONTINUALLY
TEASING AND
CHALLEGING THEM.

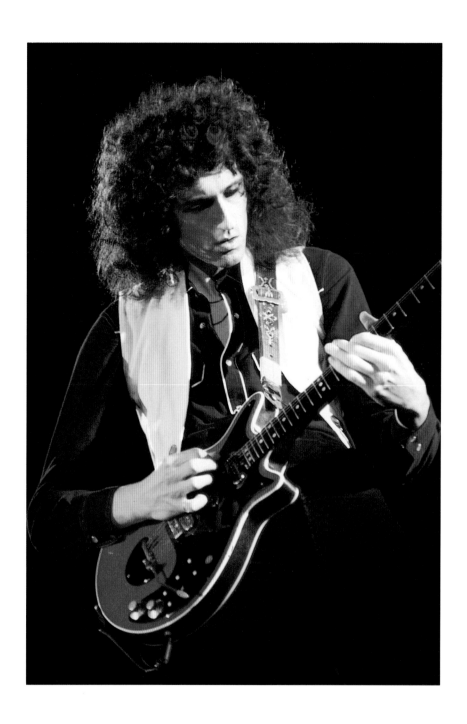

'BACK CHAT'.

**FREDDIE TREATS
THE AUDIENCE TO
A RARE
IMPERSONATION
OF THIN LIZZY'S
PHIL LYNOTT.**

JOHN DEACON
CONTRIBUTED NOT
ONLY A SOLID
RHYTHM BUT
ALSO A SOUND
HEAD FOR
BUSINESS.

'BOHEMIAN
RHAPSODY' – THE
BAND LEFT THE
STAGE DURING
THE OPERATIC
SECTION,
RETURNING FOR
THE ROCK
CRESCENDO IN A
BLINDING BLAZE
OF LIGHT.

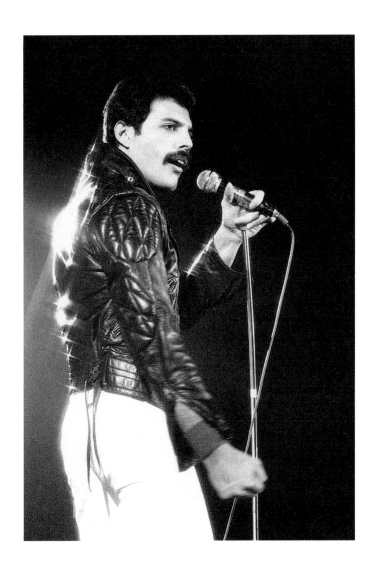

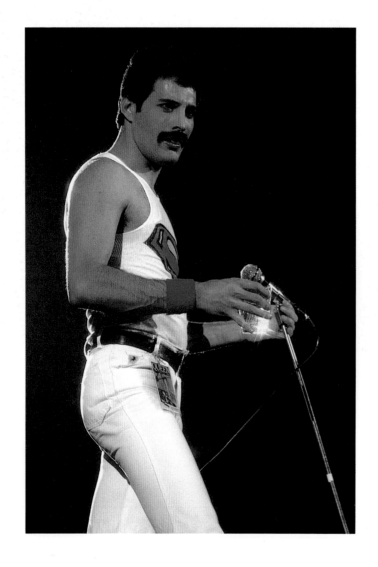

THE
LAST
T

T OUR

FREDDIE SAT ON MY
CAMERA CASE ON
THE TERRACE OF HIS
PRESIDENTIAL SUITE
OVERLOOKING THE
DANUBE AS HE AND
BRIAN REHEARSED A
HUNGARIAN FOLK
SONG FOR THEIR
PERFORMANCE AT
BUDAPEST'S
NEPSTADION.

FREDDIE CHECKS
THE ACOUSTICS AT
BUDAPEST'S
NEPSTADION,
AND REHEARSES
THE HUNGARIAN
FOLK SONG HE IS
TO SING AT
TONIGHT'S SHOW
– WHICH, WITH
AN ATTENDANCE
OF 80,000, WAS
THE BIGGEST EVER
IN THE EASTERN
BLOC. WHEN HE
SANG THE SONG
THAT NIGHT, HE
HAD NOTES
WRITTEN ON THE
PALM OF HIS
HAND!

IN PARIS, AT THE
HIPPODROME DE
VINCENNES, THE
AUDIENCE
WAITING OUTSIDE
THE GATES WERE
TREATED TO THE
RARE SOUND OF
QUEEN SOUND-
CHECKING ON
STAGE. THEY
WOULD HAVE
HEARD, FOR
INSTANCE, 'IN THE
LAP OF THE
GODS', NOT
INCLUDED IN THE
SET FOR MANY
YEARS.

THE AUDIENCE
FOLLOWED THE
RITUALISTIC
HANDCLAP FROM
THE PROMOTIONAL
VIDEO DURING THE
CHORUS OF 'RADIO
GAGA'. IT WAS
THIS THAT MADE
ME REALISE THAT
QUEEN HAD
CLAIMED THE
AUDIENCE AS THEIR
OWN AT LIVE AID.

**FREDDIE MERCURY,
WHO AS A
CHARACTER
VEERED BETWEEN
THE SHY AND THE
OUTRAGEOUS,
WAS ONE OF THE
GREATEST LIVE
PERFORMERS
EVER, AND THE
WRITER OF
'BOHEMIAN
RHAPSODY',
'LOVE OF MY
LIFE', 'WE ARE
THE CHAMPIONS'
AND 'KILLER
QUEEN'.**

**ROGER'S
DRUMBEAT ALERTED
THE AUDIENCE TO
AN IMMINENT
RENDITION OF THE
ORIGINAL VERSION
OF 'WE WILL ROCK
YOU'.**

FREDDIE WOULD
GAIN FINAL
CONTROL OF THE
CROWD BY
TALKING TO THEM
JOKINGLY, AND
THEN DRAGGING
THEM THROUGH
THE MUSICAL
SCALES UNTIL
THEY COULD NO
LONGER REACH
THE NOTES AND
HE EMERGED IN
COMMAND. ON
THE LAST TOUR HE
WOULD THEN
LAUNCH INTO
'HAMMER TO
FALL'.

OF ALL THE
GUISES IN WHICH
I PHOTOGRAPHED
FREDDIE, IT WAS
THE CROWN-AND-
ROBES COSTUME
THAT HE WAS
MOST INSISTENT I
CAPTURE IN ALL
ITS SPLENDOUR. I
THINK HE FELT
THAT THIS WAS
THE ULTIMATE IN
QUEEN THEATRE.